Memories From The Past
Dreams For The Future

Saint Anastasia Catholic School
8th Grade Class 2015/16

Memories From The Past
Dreams For The Future

Copyright © 2016 Saint Anastasia Catholic School

XMS Publishing
1391 NW St Lucie West Blvd, Suite 247
Port St Lucie, FL 34986

ISBN: 0692698191
ISBN-13: 978-0692698198

Published in the United States of America

Dedicated to the

Class of 2016...

*May you always encounter wonderful, supportive
people in each of your lives.*

Treat each day as a true gift from God.

A Warm Welcome and Blessing

To the young and aspiring future authors, poets and writers; when it comes to dreams, they can come true. Be prudent in your "wants," be aware of your "deepest desire" and when properly confirmed in your true desire; seek with all your heart, the One who placed that desire within you. It has been a gift for me to watch God transform your heart, mind and soul throughout your time at St. Anastasia. Stay close to God, the Sacraments and remember to take the time to be aware, that God is aware of you.

Fr. Richard E. George II, Pastor

Table of Contents - 8ᵗʰ Grade Authors

Forward
<u>Student Portfolios</u>

By Dr. Hoeffner, Principal

What a wonderful collection of student creativity, critical thinking, and literary talent this collection has become! The children of St. Anastasia Catholic School are such a miracle of creation. The education at our school is truly a tapestry of unique gifts and learning opportunities. The school has begun using digital student portfolios to showcase work like this, and to share information with one another about our students' success and progress. These portfolios will also seek to assess how our students are aspiring to accomplish their dreams and goals, and the goals that parents and teachers have set for them. As a community we have created a profile to assist us on outlining what a graduate of St. Anastasia Catholic School should be like. We appreciate the team effort that must occur between the home, the church, and the school to accomplish what our community desires for our graduates. We want the community to be aware that this ambitious profile below is guiding our path in the development of the whole child.

<u>The Profile of a Graduate of St. Anastasia Catholic School</u>

We the parents and teachers of St. Anastasia Catholic School would like each of our graduating eighth graders to be a:

(Religious/Spiritual) **Faith-filled Leader who:**

- Seeks out God in prayer, service, evangelization, and worship.

- Understands how to use the bible and Youth Catechism to inspire and inform his/her faith.

- Knows how to apply human and theological virtues and can defend what he/she believes.

- Strives for a deepened respect and appreciation for goodness, truth, and beauty.

(Intellectual) **Reflective and Critical Thinker who:**

- Demonstrates mastery in all of the academic disciplines and social readiness for high school.
- Uses the latest technology and information to proficiently solve complex problems.
- Frequently asks: what, why, and how and applies the knowledge that is gained to serve God and the community.
- Listens, speaks, reads, and writes effectively and creatively.

(Social/Emotional) **Global Citizen who:**

- Respects others and takes pride in his/her personal appearance, family, and school.
- Respects and cares for all life and God's creation as a responsible steward of life.
- Demonstrates how he/she is accountable to his/herself, to God, and to the community.
- Understands his/her unique talents, challenges, and learning style and develops personal goals.
- Develops basic life skills, social etiquette, and the ability to adapt to change.
- Stands up to peer pressure and makes good choices with help from God, family, and community.

(Physical) **Healthy and Balanced Teen who:**

- Participates in extracurricular activities and exhibits good sportsmanship and teamwork.
- Recognizes the benefits of a healthy lifestyle and makes choices that support the value of his/her life and others.

Preface

ENCOUNTERING GOD AND ONE ANOTHER

Our school focus this year was about how and when we encounter God. I believe that we do that many times on a daily basis as we encounter one another.

My students have so many opportunities to encounter each other, but are those small moments in time productive, rich, and filled with God's love?

To begin to make these encounter moments become more, my students decided to write about a past memory or a hope for the future.

Looking back from where you came or looking ahead to where you are going may be a small way to make all of your encounters in life more beneficial to yourself.

Mrs. Barbara D'Amato

8th grade Language Arts Teacher

Saint Anastasia School 2015/16

Gwen Anderson

Imagine… Imagine if you could fly a plane and be your own pilot, jump from the tallest building and live, or even zip line across a river with crocodiles below you. Although the these things sound adventurous and audacious, they are not for me. A bucket list is fun to have, but mine would me like this one. It would be like…traveling the world, going to college, and flying in a helicopter.

Traveling the world looks like so much fun, but I don't just want to travel the world; I want to learn about as much as I can, meet as many people as I can, and enjoy the simple pleasures of the world. History has always been my favorite subject and to learn about the history of Greece or Africa from the place that history originated from would be a great honor to me. I would hate to have to miss a great opportunity like that.

Yea… "college." I know, it sounds like no fun at all and who wants to go back to school after high school, but I feel that college helps a lot through our daily lives. I've seen it! I've seen those who go to college have a better education than those who skip out on college. I want to go to college because I want an education, and I find that learning new things fascinates me.

Helicopters. Yes, I have never ridden in a helicopter before, and I would love to experience this for myself and find out how truly amazing it is to fly up in the air and see the world underneath me. Most of my friends have experienced this thrill and they say it's awesome, but is it as amazing as everyone really says it is? Hopefully, I'll find out soon.

There you go -- my bucket list! I'm not like most people; I'm not dangerous and daring, but I sure know what I want to do in my life and I hope I get to do those things!

Angeli Assaly

Canada

The colorful leaves falling, children building snowmen, and flowers growing in the warm sun. Family barbecues and playing outside with my friends sound fantastic. My favorite memories I remember in Canada.

Leaves are falling and a chilly breeze is going through the air. It's fall. People are raking up their leaves and kids are jumping in them and having a lot of fun. I miss doing that with my sister Chloe and my brother Chad. We would go over to my neighbor's, Amanda, and slide and play in the vibrantly red and brown leaves. After, we would go inside and watch a movie. There is so much you can do in fall!

Winter comes and everything is cold and icey. Pretty snowflakes falling from the sky making thick snow covering the ground. This is my favorite season; my family would all go outside and build snowmen and make forts. After the forts were built, we would get our snowballs ready and have a snowball fight. We would invite are friends over and play manhunt in the snow. After all the outdoor fun, we would go inside and drink hot chocolate. I miss all of that plus skating on ice and eating beaver tails which is a yummy dessert in Canada.

Spring is next and all the flowers and trees grow back and a nice breeze goes through the air again. Sometimes during the week it would rain and be windy too. I would go outside and take walks with my sister and go to the park. My family would have barbecues and go on hikes. My mom, sister, and I would go to the apple orchard and pick apples and then go on the hayride; it was a lot of fun!

So many memories I can think about. I miss all the seasons and can't wait to go back to Canada soon. I miss all my friends and family and can't wait to have family barbecues and hang out with my friends again.

Lillyanna Bienz

Dear Future Self,

I hope you're well, healthy, and you have long curly hair by now. You have to realize that life is short and every second counts. You need to get off your lazy bum and stop watching Netflix! Please try to strive towards a successful job, but listen to me and start checking off your bucket list.

Obviously a bucket list is all about doing things before you die. As insane as this may sound, I think the first thing on your list that should be completed is conquering your biggest fear. Just like when we were little and we would go to the fair during the summer. We would always go on the scariest ride so that all the other rides in the fair are a breeze. That means it's time to go shark cage diving Lilly, and don't die yet, because there's more on the list. Now that that fear is out of the way, prepare yourself to go skydiving with Alivia or your bestie. Bring a GoPro or whatever awesome technology they have now. Wake up to a beautiful view in a loft in the city. Live with friends for a little while in your loft and share ideas on how to own the world. Be part of a dance crew and live it up, but don't injure your legs because you'll need them for cross country, marathons, and track meets. While you're at it get your favorite running shoes signed by Usain Bolt; you'll make your past self-proud.

Clear sparkling water on a beautiful beach sounds great, but swimming in the Bahamas with pigs is a must! Pigs are your favorite animal, don't deny it. Grab your swimsuit and go on vacation. Keep traveling and visit the black sand beach in the southern part of Iceland. After that please own a munchkin kitten - they are so adorable. Then make a beach themed wedding cake with three tiers or more. I could go on forever adding to this list, but I'll end right here with meeting the queen of the world, Beyoncé.

Love,
Lilly

P.S. Learn to make macaroons, this will be appreciated.

Brooke Botterbusch

Dear Future Self,

Isn't it weird that right now I'm sitting in my language arts class writing this? I can't predict what your life might be like, but hopefully you're living somewhere really cool and you have a big family.

Eighth grade year is halfway done. After eighth grade, I will go to John Carroll High School. Hopefully high school will be super fun. Do you remember the first place you drove when you got your car? What was the first thing you did when you turned eighteen?

For college, I want to go to FSU. But I wonder where I actually will go for college. What are some things you regret? What is your job? I don't know what I want to be yet. Hopefully what your job is fun!

What are some your biggest accomplishments? What was it like graduating high school? I bet it was a bittersweet feeling. What is the best thing about being an adult? What is the most important thing in your life right now?

Hopefully you're reading this letter. I hope your life is everything you wanted.

From,

Brooke

Pablo Bregolat

Future Goals

Hover boards, flying cars, no not that future, your future. I want to graduate from a good college. When college comes to an end, I want to be a successful contractor with a wonderful family. I want to have a big house on the beach or lake.

I want to go to a division one college, and I want to play baseball. I also want to study to become a contractor. I am going to study hard so I can have a good job and a nice house, also so I can spend time with my kids and send them to a good school. I want to be able to have a big house on the water so I can teach my kids how to fish. I will work hard so I won't have to work two jobs, and I can treat my family to dinner at least once a week.

I want to retire and spend the rest of my life with my wife. We are going to move to the Florida Keys. I will fish for fun and go snorkeling with my wife. The Florida Keys is my favorite place in Florida, that is why I want to retire and move there. I am going to live a happy life in the Florida Keys.

From,

Pablo

Jacob Krauza

My Fantastic Bucket List

I have an exciting bucket list! Since I have a lot on my list, I'll shorten it down to my top three. The first thing on my bucket list is to attend a good college. My second is to go fishing in Canada for tuna. The last item on my bucket list is to go on a cruise to Alaska.

Going to college costs a lot of money and is very important to attend. College is at the top of my bucket list because it's very important for your future. If you go to a good college, your parents would be very proud. Colleges have a lot of activities like sports and many different subjects. The teachers that teach in college are very well trained so you would have a good education and future if you go to college.

Fishing in Canada is my second thing to do on my bucket list. I love to fish. The most popular fishing in Canada is tuna because they get a lot bigger there than in anywhere else. Fishermen love catching these big fish. A tuna in Canada will feed your family for a lot of days because of its size. I hope I can do it one day to cross it off my list.

My last thing to do on my bucket list is to take a cruise to Alaska. I have heard from a lot of relatives that it's a site you will never forget. Seeing the whales and glaciers would be just amazing, you can also take a helicopter ride to the top of a glacier. A cruise to Alaska will be amazing so that's why it's one of my top three.

That is my bucket list. I have a lot more, but I just listed the top three. I hope you achieve your bucket list, and I hope yours helps you in the future.

Abbey Capezza

After Graduation

I am currently an eighth grader at St. Anastasia School, and soon I will be graduating to John Carroll High School. It will be sad to leave St. Anastasia. In high school, I will work hard in my academics so that I may do well in the future. I plan to play the sports of volleyball and basketball. After graduation life will change; I hope to make that change positive.

It will be sad to leave St. Anastasia. This school is where I grew up, beginning at the age of three. Knowing that I won't be attending this school makes me sad, but I know John Carroll will be a good change. After graduation, it will feel different. Some students will be attending different schools, and we will all meet new people. Whatever happens, I plan to make the best of it.

In high school, I will work hard in my academics so that I may do well in the future. Doing well in high school leads to a great college. A great college leads to a good career, and I think having a good career is really important in life. Doing well in academics really has so many positive effects. Every step of the way, I will strive for the best.

Finally, after graduation, I plan to play the sports of volleyball and most likely, basketball. Not only will I be getting good exercise, but I will also be able to get competitive and challenge myself. I think I am going to really enjoy playing these sports at John Carroll; although, I will miss playing volleyball and basketball at St. Anastasia.

There are definitely great things about graduating, but I know as I grow older, I will miss St. Anastasia more and more every day. We may think that graduating is the end of something, but really, it's a start to something even bigger. I've had so many great moments and memories at St. Anastasia and after graduation, I can't wait to make more.

Kate Capezza

Angel Back in Heaven

There are certain moments that can change someone's life forever. When my great-grandmother died, the lives of every person that knew her changed. Grandma Jean was a kind and loving person; she could always put a smile on my face, and she became the example that I want to follow. While she is in heaven today, I realize all of the lives she has touched and changed. She has made me want to become a better version of myself every day.

She always had a loving personality with a kind attitude. Grandma Jean would always bake and satisfy the people who got the chance to enjoy her delicious foods. She is known for saying "many hands make light work." She would always think of other people before she ever thought of herself. She loved her family and was a great parent, grandmother, and definitely an amazing great- grandmother.

A smile can add so much to a person. Whenever I would see her smile, a smile would appear on my face right away. She made others happy even when they weren't before. Whether it was by a joke or just by eating chocolate with us, she could always make me happy. Just her smile alone could light up the entire room.

To this day, I want to follow Grandma Jean. She lived as a true child of God and led everyone that knew her more towards His plan. She is a role model for me now and always will be. She lived until the age of ninety-nine, and she didn't waste one day. She found and brought out the best in everyone.

When my great-grandmother passed away it definitely changed my life. I didn't like seeing everyone in my family sad but we all knew she was in heaven, doing better than she ever was before. She was always kind and loving. She could always put a smile on my face even by her smile alone, and she is my example. Every other characteristic that she has is indescribable because there are definitely way too many. Grandma Jean was the kind of person that I think everyone should have gotten to know.

Sam Cardosi

Bucket List

Some people think it is crazy, but skydiving seems fun to me. That's one thing on my bucket list. Other things on my bucket list are flying a plane and driving a tank. Crazy, right??!! Well, it just sounds fun to me!

Skydiving is a worldwide hobby, and it is on my bucket list. Think about it--falling out of the sky being weightless. You can even do flips without jumping! Some people are terrified to try it, but to me it sounds exhilarating. Skydiving it the first thing I want to do when I get older.

I like being in the sky so flying a plane sounds fun to me too. I also like being in control, especially if I am moving very fast. Ever since I was a little kid I have wanted to fly a plane. When I grow up I want to be a pilot. If I ever become a pilot, I would do one of my favorite things all day.

Running over trees. Demolishing everything in its way. You guessed it, driving a tank. I would enjoy being in control of an almost unstoppable vehicle. That is why it is on my bucket list.

Skydiving, flying a plane, and driving a tank are just somethings I want to do before I die. To me these things are the best things to do in the world; that is why they are on my bucket list. I hope you have a bucket list so that you have goals in your life to strive for!

Randi Casalaspro

Favorite Memories

Some of my favorite memories are from when I was in school. I don't really remember anything from when I was very little, but from when I was in kindergarten here are some of my most favorite memories.

When I was in kindergarten my teacher, Miss Nicole, would always go up on her tiptoes. The class would ask her why she did that and she said it was because she used to be a ballerina. In my class Miss Nicole would make jokes and play weird games with us, and everyone would laugh and have a good time. I loved her sense of humor! In kindergarten I also met my best friend, Mariah. She was new that year and didn't have many friends, so I started to hang out with her and we became really good friends. We still talk now and have a friendship that will last forever. Kindergarten was my favorite year because I made new friends and learned many new things.

Memories are things we have for life whether they are good or bad. Most of my favorite memories are from school, and I will cherish them always. They will be with me forever.

McKenzie Christopher

MEMORIES

Memories are the best thing in my life, especially in school. A lot of memories can make you cry and make you laugh. Memories are usually the best way to explain yourself in a funny way. Memories will never be made by not doing something. Everybody I know loves memories.

I remember in third grade when Jaxon and Jacob were hanging their bags up. They were racing to the door. Jaxon apparently tripped and fell. We all turned around and Jaxon made a hole in the wall by tripping. I don't think that anybody would forget that. Memories are fun for everyone.

I know that NO one will forget the "accident" when I was in seventh grade. After the softball championship (that we lost), we still went to celebrate. We went to Applebee's to have lunch. Sarah Richmond, Brooke Botterbusch, and I went to the bathroom to take selfies. I was doing the whip in the bathroom, and slipped and fell on the dirty bathroom floor and man, it did hurt! Sarah and Brooke thought that I was faking, but I wasn't. I heard a big crack and felt it. I couldn't walk on it. I begged my mom to take me to the doctor and finally, she said ok. So off we went with my dad too. I got an X-Ray. My mom kept on saying that I just pulled a ligament, but I knew that I didn't. The doctor came in and told me and my parents that I fractured my metatarsal bone. I was so happy that I proved my mom and dad wrong, but I'm still not happy about my foot. I had to get two casts, and I absolutely hated them.

Everybody still makes fun of me for doing the whip in the bathroom and every time I go to Applebee's, I always go to the bathroom and take a picture of the spot where I fell and broke my foot. Memories are best thing that God made for us. Even if they include a broken bone or two.

Jack Leach

Crazy Birthday

I have many memories, but the one that sticks out to me the most was my twelfth birthday. I cannot remember it all, but the part that I remember best is busting my lip open. As you can imagine it was pretty scary, but it was also surprisingly fun at the same time. That's what I remember from that amazing and scary day!

The party was a blast. The kids were having fun on the water slide, and the adults were relaxing watching football. We were doing tricks so I thought it would be cool to do a front flip. Some questions were floating in my head like, " Is this too risky?" or " Could I get hurt? " but I pushed them out of my mind. I got ready and I jumped. When I was in midflight, I felt a sharp pain in my lip. When I got to the bottom, I tasted blood in my mouth. I went over to my dad and he became wide eyed. There was a hole in my lip! I was freaking out, but my dad said it was fine and that I just needed a stitch. It wasn't pleasant, but at least I had a story to tell.

As you can see it wasn't my finest birthday party. I was embarrassed when people had to sing Happy Birthday to me with my lip swollen the size of an orange. It could've been worse! At least I got back in time to eat my cake!!!

Olyvia Church

Childhood Memories

Everyone has memories; you just have to find them. Good memories and bad memories, I've had my fair share of both. I have had more good memories than bad, so I guess that makes me a lucky person. One of my greatest memories was on a Christmas Eve night when my sister, Maddie, and I started a little tradition for just the two of us.

I had gotten scared because I was sleeping by myself in a very dark room, so I ran to Maddie's bedroom and asked her if I could sleep with her that night. When she said yes I jumped into her bed and made myself comfortable. She started to read a Christmas book to me and then after we had finished the book, we became very sneaky. We went out of the room and took an extra mattress with us. We set the mattress right in front of the TV and we watched many Christmas movies like "Rudolph the Red-Nosed Reindeer" and "Here Comes Santa Claus."

When the final movie was finished we went back to the room and went to bed. We woke up at around 6:30 in the morning and in our house, we weren't supposed to come out of our rooms until 7:30 in the morning; but we went out of our rooms at 6:50. We saw tons and tons of presents! We just sat there in awe looking at the mound of presents awaiting their turn to be opened by our tiny hands. We went to our parents room and told them to wake up because it was Christmas morning. We usually wait for our Nana to come over before we open our presents, so because we couldn't wait, we called her. She came two hours earlier than she usually did. We had an amazing Christmas Day!

It has been nine years and our tradition is still going strong. Maddie moved out and I took her place as the Christmas Eve host. Maddie still comes over sometimes to take part in our little "event" and it is always a blast when she does!

Jaxon Grimes

My Bucket List

I have a lot of exciting topics on my bucket list. My top three: going to a good college, going skydiving, and going hunting in Alaska. Those are just my top favorites out of many more.

I want to go to a good college. The college I want to go to is the University of Florida. I would want to attend this school because it is close to my family and friends. The second reason why because of its amazing athletics. All my friends want to attend University of Florida too.

The second thing on my bucket list is going skydiving. I would have to wait to be older. It sounds like a cool experience. I would want to experience this in Montana.

My last thing I want to do that's on my bucket list is to go hunting in Alaska. I am a very big fan of hunting, especially for deer. It is a once in a lifetime trip to go hunting in Alaska. I would like to go hunt southwest of Alaska. I hope I can go hunting there one day.

That's my bucket list. I hope I can achieve my it one day. If you have a bucket list, I hope you can achieve yours too.

Kylee Dougherty

Dear Me,

Surprise! It's me from eighth grade. By the time you read this I hope you have graduated high school with good grades, completed dual enrollment, and that you're finishing up six years (or more) of college. Other than your career and educational life, I hope you have accomplished many goals. For example, trying a different sport and/or trying to get a scholarship.

I hope you made it into Embry-Riddle for space physics or aerospace engineering. I also wanted you to go to Syracuse University to study life science and occasionally attend football games. I hope they're are playing well and are fortunate to make it into the national championship. After college, I plan to stay in New York and live out my career. You're probably laughing right now of how non compos mentis I sound. Hope you're doing well.

Kylee

Sara Clupny

Dear Future Self,

Hello, it's me, or well you, I guess. I'd like to fantasize where your life may be now; maybe you've settled in San Francisco like you've planned. I wonder where you've traveled by now. It's so strange to think now, high school starts soon and I honestly feel like it's still 2008, I guess that's just me though. Florida is nice, I like it here. Most of the people are a lot nicer than people up north. I don't know if I'll ever warm up to the heat; however, my heart and mind are still in wintertime.

Anyway, I think I'm rambling on now, oh well. I'd love to travel after college; I hope you get to someday soon if you haven't already. Italy, Germany, Japan, Australia, etc., so many amazing cultures that I want to experience for myself one day. I'm curious as to what you've decided to go to school for, did you take mom's advice and study art? Maybe photography or theatre? Maybe you will surprise everyone and study something completely out of the blue, who knows??!!

The last few years were complicated and rough, but things are starting to look up now and I'm eager to let life happen from now on. Well this is all I have to say today, so farewell for now.

Sincerely,

Sara (2015)

Camryn Davis

School Memory

As a student at a Catholic school, it's very challenging when it comes to school work. I've had lots of memories from my two years of attending St. Anastasia Catholic School. I really love the teachers, the other students, and most importantly, the way the teachers teach and educate me to the point where I can have a greater understanding of things. It's very nice to be in a private and also a small setting school. I personally love private schools because you really get more help with all your school work, as well as homework.

My two years of experience at a Catholic school has been the bomb!!! Over all, my seventh grade year was the best due to all the nice field trips and being involved with many new things. Attending a Catholic school is better than being in a public system because you are measured by your participation and effort in your classes. At St. Anastasia, if the teachers see that you're struggling in any subject, they will get you the help that you need. Being in a Catholic school builds a better and stronger relationship with yourself and the Lord, Jesus Christ.

My seventh grade memories are the best memories, but I hope my eighth grade year memories will be even better. I want to be looked up to and be known as a young leader of St. A's. My seventh grade teacher, Ms. Smith, always tells the students that "the memory is the first to go." Leaving St. A's will be pretty sad, but I will have lots and lots of fun memories left behind. When I make it to John Carroll High

School I want to be able to say, "Hey guys, do you remember this happened in seventh grade and that happened to me in the eighth grade?" I also bet my friends and I will laugh at the great memories we've had, as well as the sharing of the memories.

In conclusion, memories are fun at times and memories can be about the worst of times. Just to think about all the fun times you had as a young teenage adult, with your friends and your family members. I remember hearing, "You aren't who you are without memories," and as soon as I heard that I went into deep thought and I began to think about my family, my friends, and most importantly, who I am and who I'm becoming in today's society.

Camron Davis

Football

During my earlier days as a young child, I've always dreamed of playing football as I got older and older. My future goal was to be a great football player and a great sportsman. As I got older and more into football, Cam Newton was the one person that I learned the game of football and the fundamentals of football and from that day, I followed Cam Newton's path.

As I have gotten older over the years, I've become more of a sports person. When I was six my mom saw me becoming a sports person; she decided to think about signing my brother and me up for a football team. When I turned ten my mom signed my brother and me up for a football team named Seminoles. When I started playing for Seminoles, my dad talked to the coach about my brother and me and ever since that game, I became starting quarterback and my brother became starting wide- receiver. As my brother and I started to become a big part of the football team, we started to work harder and harder at our positions and became great at it.

Over time, my brother and I got better. Our coach told the team that our first game was this Saturday and the whole team was pumped up for the first game. When that Saturday came, everyone said they were pumped up for the game, but everyone really was nervous and had butterflies in their stomachs. When we got in the locker room, our couch gave a speech about how we could do it and we could win today's game and many more; and then everyone was pumped up and ready for the game. Everyone put on their equipment and put on their jerseys and cleats, and they were ready to play the game

When we were ready to play, kickoff team and kick return team got on, but our team was on offense first so we received the ball. When we got the ball we got plenty of yards and that's when the offense got on the field. Since my brother and I had starting positions, we already knew we were going do something good. The first play of the game my brother went out for a fly and I had time in the pocket, and I threw it to my brother who was wide open for my first touchdown of the first season.

The older I got, the more athletic I became. Sports became a natural hobby for me as I got older. I love to challenge myself and work hard at what I do the best, and football is a sport that I know I have to excel and work hard in to be the very best.

Julia DeMott

Family Vacations

Family vacations are the best way to spend your summer. We've visited amusement parks around Florida, we've taken road trips around the United States, and we've travelled on twenty-six hour plane rides across the globe. Whether it is in Florida or on the other side of the world, time spent with family is simply the best!

Two full hours of naps, singing, laughing, and telling stories in the car is a great way to start off our Disney World family tradition. Since my parents had employee privileges back then, my whole family could enjoy a nice weekend at Disney for free. My favorite park was Magic Kingdom because I got to see all of my best friends at the time: Mickey, Minnie, Pluto, and especially Chip and Dale. As the years went by, I began to like Epcot more and I started looking forward to driving my own car after riding Test Track over ten times in a row. My cousins and I all loved Epcot too because of Around the World, where we could eat crepes from France while riding a Viking boat in Norway. Disney World is never a bore with your family!

Being only ten years old in Las Vegas was very challenging for me, considering that I was not allowed in certain areas of the hotels, even with an adult by my side. It was fun having my freedom restored in Fremont, where I was allowed to go anywhere I wanted. We all walked around and ate gelatos in the Bellagio after having a fancy buffet dinner at the M Resort. Then, we climbed up Red Rock

Mountain and even drove to Utah to visit Zion National Park. I had an amazing time in Las Vegas, but maybe I would enjoy it even more if I was about ten years older. That didn't really matter at the time because I was having a blast with my family who won almost $100 during the trip -- you might know how!

Flying on airplanes can be both scary yet soothing, from the popping of your ears to the beautiful scenery above the clouds. For over twenty-six hours, the plane ride from the United States to the Philippines was very exciting. I've only flown there once, but it was such a great experience. I suffered from severe jet lag when I landed in Manila because it was two in the morning when we got there, and we should have been asleep. I was not fully accustomed to the Philippine time until after a full week. I never believed my mom when she said I had more close cousins than classmates, but that quickly changed after I met all forty of them! In the Philippines, I went zip-lining over an erupting volcano, fed and rode an elephant, and met a whole lot of family I have never seen before. You could say I had a good time!

"Money spent on travel is never wasted." (Author unknown) I love going places with my family, whether it's around Florida, around the United States, or around the globe. I think everyone should go places with family to strengthen the bond between the members. So, where will you go?

Devan Fischbeck

Dear Me,

I know you have high expectations for your life. I want to be successful and have a great family. I also would like to become a teacher. Although all these things might not become true, I will strive for them. You are probably laughing at how untrue this is, but keep going for your goals!

Never let anyone bring you down. There are people that are going to try to dampen your spirit, but keep your head high. Take your education seriously and do well in school. Get a good job and be successful! Remember, you can do anything you set your mind to.

Most importantly, go have fun! Do not be too serious! Here I am, an eighth grader telling you what to do, but I am you! Take my advice and you will do wonderfully! I cannot wait to see you!

Love,

Devan

Rick-Paul Jean Simon

Dear Future Self,

I am assuming you are in your thirties; you're getting older and planning to start a business or may already have one. I wonder if you have changed at all, hopefully if you did change, it was in a good way and not in a bad way. We worked way too hard to just throw your life away; it's not worth it. Do you live in a nice apartment or house? I hope we went to a good college. I hope you stayed out of trouble.

About your wife, I hope you found someone who truly loves you and now have kids. Always treat her with respect no matter what because it's the right thing to do. Remember what mom said, never lay your hand on a girl because it's not right. Always listen to her because a happy wife is a happy life. I know that's what we want. Never cheat on her because it's wrong. Do that and life should be good.

Dude, by now you should have multiple sports cars or may have built your own. It must be super-fast or what's the point? We need to have the best car ever. I will be so happy if you have the Agera r; it's our dream car. I can just hear that car in my head right now and feel it too. Cars have been in my blood since the day I was born so let's keep it that way. You should make a one of kind car for our mom and dad because we love them.

I know we're not the best at math, and mom and dad say without math you can't be engineer. I hope that didn't affect our chance of starting a company. I know it's not going to be easy, but I know you did it because your Rick-Paul. Don't forget to give back too. I want you to start a Christmas program that gives presents to kids who don't get any. Every kid deserves Christmas presents.

Do have kids and make sure they stay healthy. Take care of them. Make sure you put them in private school; we have been going to private school for a long time. Love them a lot and put them in sports. I hope you try your best not to miss a game. Be there. It means a lot, trust me. I know you're a hard worker, and I know you can do it. I hope you see this letter.

From,

Rick-Paul

Sophia Glenn

Traveling

There are many places on earth to visit, almost too many to count. When I grow up I want to travel to new places and experience new things. My three dream vacations would be going to Hawaii, Iceland, and Australia. I can't imagine what my life would be like if I traveled to these places.

The place I want to visit the most is Hawaii. Hawaii is such a beautiful place with gorgeous waters. They have many interesting things like active volcanoes. Hawaii consists of many small islands and is a great place for swimming and snorkeling. I would love the experience of traveling over the intimidating Pacific Ocean to this exotic place.

Another magnificent place I would love to travel to is Iceland. This beautiful place consists of black sand beaches, glaciers, and waterfalls. This is also known as the Republic of Iceland and many people live there. If I ever had the chance to go to this amazing place, I would love to go hiking and experience the amazing views.

The last place that I dream of visiting is Australia. This extraordinary place is known for its large Outback. The Outback includes many interesting animals like kangaroos. Not only is Australia known for its cool animals, but also their Opera House in Sydney, Australia. If I ever go to the "Outback," I hope to see many animals.

There are many options to choose from if you could

travel anywhere you wanted. From the kangaroos in Australia, the green fields in Iceland, to the clear water in Hawaii; they are all very diverse. All of these places are amazing, and I hope to visit them one day.

Anthony D'Alessio

Dear Future Self,

 I hope I am something like I describe. First, I hope I have a good family and a great job that I like. That is what I hope I am like in the future.

I would like to have a great family with a great wife and beautiful kids. Then, I want to be close to my parents so my kids can enjoy them every day like I did. I hope my family is something like I described.

Next, I hope I have a great job that has to do with the ocean because that is what I love. I hope I make enough money to have extra spending money. I would like to have a friend working around me so it makes work easier. I hope my job is like that.

That is what I wish my future self is like - having a great family and an amazing job that I love.

From,

Anthony

Jennifer Kaminski

My Goals in the Future

Now I'm only in eighth grade, but I really kind of know what I would like to do later in life. But sometimes, I also don't know for sure because I haven't yet made my mind. I hope when I do I know, they will be good choices.

I would like to go to Alabama State or FSU. I have always loved those two colleges just because they are beautiful campuses. I would like to major in would be an oncologist because I like helping people and caring for people.

Later in my life, I think that I would be married. I would still have a lot of goals to accomplish like I would like to have my degree in medical science, like I said I want to be an oncologist. But I would also have this other little goal like meeting famous people.

That is what I hope my future turns out to be like. I can't wait to grow up and finally have a good job and set goals for myself. I would like to have other little goals like having to meet other new people also to do new exciting things.

That's what I would like to do with my future, and I hope that it will happen.

Brandon Jones

My Bucket List

I have a lot of things on my bucket list. The things I listed are a lot of very great things to do every day in my life.

My favorite things are on my bucket list. My favorite goal is making it into the major leagues in baseball. I want to do that because I love to play baseball. I also think that baseball is a great sport to see with family and friends. That is my best and favorite thing on my bucket list.

My second best thing on my bucket list is that I want to play tackle football. I love to play this because I love to play the sport too. When I play football, I feel so alive. I also get to learn how to do and play the sport too.

The third to best thing on my bucket list is to go to college. I want to go to college because I want to get a great education to get a great job. And hopefully, I can go play sports at college too. If I would be able to do these things, it would be great!

Arthur Larochelle

Dear Future Me,

I hope that you read this message because I wrote this exactly for you. I wrote this is to make you have some advice and lessons. Listen very well.

I'm going to begin with action. Our worst action is when we get mad. I'm actually happy that our reactions of anger never showed up at school. When you get mad at anything your feelings come out of you, but you have to stop the anger somehow. I know sometimes they just bust out of you; what I have to say is that when they want to come out, let it go.

Problem, when you have a problem don't kill yourself trying to solve it yourself -- that's why your family's there. One other thought is that sometimes you just don't focus on anything, even other people, like your family. Take good care of everyone and your surroundings. Don't give up, don't let go; you're still there. You change a lot over time and will get more used to life, that's great.

Make your life the easiest as possible for you and others to live in. Be a good boy and have self-control, please. In your life always remember your family. I wish for you to have a good day and year living with God.

From,

Arthur

Grace Lamb

My Fantastical Bucket List

Skydiving, wrestling a shark, or flying a helicopter. All of these things are on a "normal" bucket list. Mine is a bit more tame. Before I die, I want to go to college, become a vet, and go to New York City, just to name a few.

When I go to college, I will train to become a veterinarian for dogs and horses. First, I will graduate from high school with my dual enrollment. Then, I will hopefully go to the University of Florida, even though I'm not a fan of football. I will then spend the next four to five years in college, to then graduate college when I'm about twenty- three or twenty-four. That is basically half of my life goals! Yay!

Now for the other half of my life goals. When I become a vet, I will mainly work with dogs and horses because I have a lot of experience with each. For my patients, I will have water therapy. Water therapy is basically having an animal swim in a pond or swimming pool to heal a broken bone without having them put any weight on it. Now on to random goals!

Last but not least, I will go to New York City. Now, this is probably the most exciting thing on my bucket list. When I go to New York, I will go to the very top of the Empire State Building and look down at all of the little tiny ant-sized people. Then, I will probably go to the public library. I also hope to go to the Belmont Racetrack and see the thoroughbreds.

All in all, it's not such a bad bucket list, if not a little boring. Let's review. Three things on my bucket list: go to college, become a vet, and go to New York. Woohoo!

Gabrielle Levesque

Dear Future Self,

Congrats! You found this letter and have not lost it yet. First off, I hope you grew taller and can finally do a pull-up. Other than that, I want you to go to a great college and graduate successfully. From there, I hope you have a beautiful family with a loving husband and two children (a boy and a girl). I cannot wait to see what progress you have made.

I hope you had a great volleyball career in college and make sure you teach your kids how to play too. Do not let your busy work life get in the way of spending time with your family. Vacation is a must; go to amazing places like Bora Bora and many more. Also, do not hesitate to travel because you love it! I vision you in a big house by the beach where you can watch the sunset each night and take super cute pictures with your family. Stay in touch with your best friends too because some of your best memories are with them. You can all take your kids to the park and talk about everything going on with life.

I know things might get tough, but what part of life is easy? Just remember the phrase "never give up." Even if things hit the ultimate low, keep your head up because you are strong, confident, and independent. Go to Mass every Sunday because you need God in your life. Also, take care of your children. Even when nothing is going your way think, "Your kids need you so stay strong and don't give up." Until we see each other again.

Love, your eighth grade self,

Gabrielle

Kaitlin Mathey

My Family Vacation

I love going on family vacations so I can gain a whole bunch of irreplaceable memories. I love going on trips with my family!

Family vacations make the best memories. I love going on relaxing vacations with my family. One time I went on vacation with my mom, dad, and cousin. We went to Disney and Universal. This was when I was eight. I was finally tall enough to ride all of the rides, but unfortunately, my cousin wasn't. So he got mad, and I couldn't ride any of the rides I wanted. Chris ended up crying so we had to leave.

There was another time when I was with my cousin Ava, we went to Epcot! We went to all the countries and tried their desserts. We went to France and got crepes; they were delicious! Next, we went to America and tried funnel cake, that was good too! We also went to Mexico and tried fried ice cream; it was disgusting! Then, we tried Norwegian Chocolate--it was the best chocolate I have ever had in my life! We also rode the Viking ship ride; it was so much fun even though it was super scary!

Family trips are priceless. The memories you make, the people you spend it with, and all the fun you have. All of it is priceless, every single second. My favorite family trip was when my mom, dad, grandma, grandpa, and I went to Disney; we had so much fun and made so many memories. I had a lot of fun! I wouldn't have traded it for the world.

I love going on family vacations! If I got to choose I would make every vacation a family vacation. They really do make the best memories!

Nicolas Macias

My Bucket List

I have a bucket list that I would like to complete before I die. I want to travel to amazing places and do great things. I will talk about what is amazing, things that will encourage you.

Have you ever heard the word YOLO, (You, Only, Live, Once)? I love Europe and that is where I want to go. I want to go to Seal Island off the coast of Africa so I can get some pictures and see sharks jump out of the water and eat the seals. I want to go skydiving. I would want to go to Europe and visit all the enchanted things that are there to see. While I'm there I would want to go to a Real Madrid soccer game and see Cristiano Ronaldo. They say that the games are huge and they are very fun to go to.

Second thing is to go to Seal Island and watch the Great Whites eat them. When I watch "Shark Week" on Discovery, there it is, Seal Island. They say there are huge sharks there that get up to twenty feet long. Most of the seals are cautious when they are in the water.

My last thing is to go skydiving. I want to feel the wind blow me away and be up three thousand feet in the air. This is a popular one that everyone will want to do.

That is it. I can't wait till the day comes that I can have these exciting adventures!

Orla McQuaid

Dear Future Orla,

Are you living in New York like we always dreamed of? Did you get to up-do lofts in the city? Maybe this is too far ahead. How was high school? Who was your favorite teacher and your friends? Are they the same friends from middle school or different ones? Where did you go when you first got your car? I hope you are loving life!

Right now I'm in eighth grade at Saint Anastasia School. My homeroom teacher is Mrs. D'Amato and she is probably my favorite teacher upstairs. I enjoy visiting my sister in Tampa. She attends the University of Tampa. I plan to go there when I'm older. For graduate school I'll probably go up north to New York.

My dream in eighth grade right now is to attend John Carroll High School. I would like to get into honor classes there and be in the top ten group. I would love to be accepted into the University of Tampa. I have experience with different colleges from my sister. Both of us agree on loving University of Tampa. In high school I really want to focus on my studies, but also to have a break once in a while. I want to join many different clubs, be involved with sports, and have fun with my best friends. I hope you enjoyed your time at Saint Anastasia School and John Carroll. Keep on dreaming! I know "we" will go far.

Lots of love from your past self,
Orla McQuaid

Keegan Molloy

Disney Tradition

When my parents married, they wanted to create a family tradition that their children could repeat. They believed that Walt Disney World had a strong chance of remaining the same. It brought the same wonderful Christmas year after year. They assumed their children could go there as adults and enjoy Christmas as we did as children. They also supposed that we could show our own children a little bit of our childhood Christmas. My early family started the tradition with staying nights in a van and tents at the campground. We got an R.V. when we lived on an Air Force base. We moved to the log cabins when lost the R.V. in hurricane Katrina.

We enjoined the Christmas story and the festive singing in the Disney parks. The Osborn family lights show was one of our favorites. In the Magic kingdom, there was fake snow, holiday outfits and shows, and toy soldiers that almost always made us laugh. Some Christmases we didn't even have to spend in the parks. One thing that we did out of the parks that was really fun was riding monorails, especially when we got to go in the front car. Making cookies at certain hotels always ended with a tasty treat and loads of smiles. The campground was the real thing that we had to do when we were in Disney World.

The Fort Wilderness Campground has a lot of nice components like s'mores, golf carts, movies, and sing along with blankets by the fires. The trading posts had other cool stuff like large checkers, colorful rocks, and fake guns. There was lots of things that kids can do to keep occupied. I always enjoyed riding in the golf cart when my brother would drive and not only because he drove like crazy. The cool breeze of December blowing on my faces while I was in the golf cart was always the thing I loved the most. Now, every time I feel that chilly breeze blow against my skin, I get goosebumps and a stream of memories that curves my mouth into a smile.

Matthew Miller

Bucket List

Ever since I was little, I have always wanted to be a country star, but that is just one of the items on my fantastic bucket list. I have a long list of items on my bucket list. I need to have some fun before I get too old.

As I said before, I have always wanted to be a country star. I would also like to go to the Olympics and win a gold medal in swimming. I want to be an actor. I want to go skydiving. I want to ride in a helicopter and a stunt airplane. I want to become a great cook. I want to visit Costa Rica. I have always wanted to be a spy. I want to learn how to free dive up to thirty feet deep. I want to create a product to make people's lives easier. Finally, I want to become famous.

A bucket list, as you can see, is a great thing to have. It is a fun way to organize your dreams. After all, I need to have some fun before I get too old.

Abhi Patel

Future Goals

Everyone has a bucket list, but I think I have a long list for my bucket list. My top items on my bucket list are going skydiving, going to Oxford University or a good college, and becoming a software engineer. My fourth item is to become a professional gamer and make videos on YouTube when I grow up.

Going skydiving is so much fun. The thrill must be amazing. I want to feel the air in my hair and the excitement of jumping out of the plane. I want to experience the anticipation of going on the plane and jumping. I always wanted to go skydiving, and I hope to go in the future.

Going to Oxford University when I grow up is another dream of mine. I want to become a software engineer. If I don't go to Oxford, I at least want to go to the University of Florida. I am really good at computers and electronics so I think I would be good at becoming a software engineer.

Finally, I would love to become a YouTuber and make amazing content for people. I would make videos about all the new games on my PlayStation. I love to play the game Destiny, Star Wars Battlefront, or Black Ops 3 on my ps4. I would possibly make Star Wars Battlefront, and Destiny and Call of Duty and some other games as well.

So, those are my three top bucket list. I hope in the future I will be able to do all these things and much more.

Tahje Pelle

Mexico

Back in 2013, My family and I went on a trip to Cancun, Mexico. Yes, I know, I've been to Costa Rica, France, Spain, and Belgium. Mexico is the only place that I got the chance to go to with my two cousins, Ally and Jerriah. Even though we have a lot of fun in the country, it's a bit more fun out of the country. We stayed in Mexico for about six days, and I think we honestly made the most of it.

On the first day we got to Mexico, we were super excited, and could not wait to get to the resort. The resort looked great; it was tall, and right next to the beach. Once we actually went inside, we let the adults handle the checking in and walked around to check out the place. First we stayed inside and looked around. There was a bar in the center of the inside, a theater for plays, which were performed every night, and inside that theater there was another bar in the back. There was also a game room and a spa. Outside was the pool, it was huge and it was pretty much a pool linked to other pools. There were small bridges so people could get to the other side of the pool without getting wet. On the other side of the pool was the bar, which was also in the pool, but served people that were both in and out of the pool. Around the bar were tables for people to eat lunch and look at the beautiful beach behind them. We, meaning my two cousins and I, were almost at the pool every day drinking our piña coladas and having a good time. When we weren't at the pool we were either walking all around the resort or with everyone else observing Cancun.

First we went to an underwater cave. A lot of people went inside the water and swam around with the sunlight shining through above and reflecting on the water. Then, We went to Chechen Itza, a place where the Mayans used to stay. We saw the El Castillo and where the Mayans would play their ballgame which was a big spacey court. After all that, we ate where the Mayans would eat and had their type of food, which was pretty good. We also went to a mall and some outdoor markets that were nearby. When we got back to the resort, we continued what we would usually do and continued to have our fun until we had to leave.

Mexico was a good experience that I got to enjoy with my cousins. Cancun with it's pretty beaches, and all the other great things we saw, a place that I'll always remember. We all had our fun in the great and beautiful Cancun.

Saul Perez

Future Goals

Soccer is really tough. It's not the easiest sport; it takes lots of courage and skills and lots of practice. My future with soccer is getting a scholarship to college with the help of high school soccer. You have to travel to play other soccer teams and tournaments to bring home the trophies and lots of pride. Soccer can also bring you to many new friendships. Lastly, you need lots and lots practice. Hard work pays off; it shows it in the field. The better you are, the higher possibility you get if getting a scholarship. Soccer has its challenges.

First off, traveling for soccer is really fun but hard. The reasons it's good is because you get to see new towns and see every game and its new challenges along the way. Some bad things about it is that you are going to have to wake up early to go play soccer in different cities. Another thing is when you lose your game, you have to go all the way home in a bad mood.

Secondly there is a scholarship. Scholarships are really important to me. It is going to get more serious in high school, but now I'm just training to be an outstanding player on the field so the people can see me and put me in a great college. Scholarships also have to do with grades. Scholarships are really important to many soccer players.

Lastly is practice. Practice is really necessary to be an extremely talented player. You can't just pick up a soccer ball and be the best. Practice is really hard and stressful. That's what makes it perfect. Hard work does pay off. Lot and lots of hard working practice.

So my future is going big places with soccer. Either it's a scholarship or becoming a great soccer player. I believe soccer will help and bring me to success. That's my future goal.

William Picchiarini

My Future

I have a lot of crazy dreams, goals, and crazy things that I want to do. Like playing three professional sports, being president, and being an astronaut. I know that all three of these things are unlikely. If I ever get to do any of these, it would be pretty crazy. But it all starts with a dream.

My first goal is to go a Division I school and play a sport. I would like be able to play all three sports in college, and my dream college would be either Duke or Notre Dame. I would go to get a degree in some sort of space science and minor in business/entrepreneurship. I would use all four years of eligibility then declare for the draft in all three sports. It would be ideal if I was drafted by teams all in the same city so I could play all three. I'm pretty sure that would make me the first professional three sport athlete in history.

I would play football the shortest, play three years, be a WR/TE, and then retire. I want to be the leading receiver in the league and try and win a Super Bowl. I would play basketball for ten or more years, playing wing. I want to be one of the best of my time, win a couple Finals, maybe a Gold Medal, win MVP, and be top fifteen in scoring in the league every year. In baseball, I would play the longest, until I'm thirty-eight, I want to be a utility player (someone who plays all positions) and be a relief pitcher on some days. I want to win a couple Gold Gloves and Silver Sluggers and be batting champion. I want to be the best hitter ever and hit over .400 one season. I also want to join the 3,000 hits and 500 home run clubs. By the time I retire, I will be considered one of the greatest athletes ever. I would need a few years to recover.

During my sports career, I would like to get married, have a family, and have a sort of normal life. I would like to have my own shoe with Nike. I would also like to start my own small restaurant in Fort Pierce (Name TBD). When I retire from sports, I would get a job as a part time analyst for ESPN and move back home.

When I get tired of being retired, I will apply for a job at NASA and be an astronaut; I want to see what it looks like up there, I know it'll be beautiful, and I want to be in a zero gravity environment. Although by that time, I could probably just hop on one of those SpaceX rides and go up there. Or maybe, we'll be able to go to another earth-like planet. I think it would be pretty cool to go up there and see what it is like.

After I go to space, I would like to run for president. I would kind of run because the job comes with a nice retirement house. I would make some major world changes and make an effort for peace around the world. I'm not sure about other changes because that's about fifty years away from now. I probably wouldn't be elected, but it is worth the try. After that, I would officially retire and live the rest of my life traveling the world.

That would be a great life, wouldn't it? I don't think playing three sports is possible, I will be lucky enough to play one. And running for president? Lol, I don't think so. I don't know my future. I am still a kid. I am not ready to think that far down the road right now. But I can dream, and everything starts with a dream.

Jonathan Plata

Dear Jonathan,

Believe it or not, I am writing this as a thirteen year old in eighth grade. I hope you read this on your fiftieth birthday. Happy birthday to you; I hope this letter will bring a smile to you as a present from yourself.

First let me remind you what the world is like or was. Right now people call you "Bitzer" and I would explain, but it would take more than a letter. Also the economy isn't great, but we're getting along. Terrorism is a big bad thing along with abortion. Enough about all the bad stuff. Right now your grades are really good and you just got your first longboard. My favorite subject is science. My career goals are to be either a physicist or an astronomer, but maybe the future holds a different plan for me. I'm almost certain you're married by now and have kids, maybe grandkids. Maybe if we were lucky, we got our dream car and a dream house.

Don't change who you were deep down. Accomplish your goals and the things you always wanted to do. Don't forget about your family and what they did for you. Happy birthday Jonathan! Take care.

From your,

Younger, less experienced, and hilarious self-Jonathan

Abigail Austin

Letter to Self

Hello. I'm writing this letter on November 2nd 2015. The reason for this letter is to just to give you something to read when you are upset, anxious, nervous, or just needing something to read. I would like to give you not advice, but reminders of what is important. The first thing is to stay yourself, never let anyone push you down. Secondly, I would like to tell you is to keep Ella herself, don't let the bad things change her bubbly and cute personality.

One thing that I would like you to remember Abigail is to always be yourself. I know that right now things at home can be confusing and difficult, but just keep smiling no matter how hard and frustrating they are. Something else I would like to say is don't let anyone change who you are, you are perfect in every way. Lastly, I would like to say you are loved. You are loved by lots of people, your friends, family, and even people you may think don't like you. People care about you, so if you ever feel lonely, make a list in your head and think to yourself, I am loved.

In conclusion, I would just like to say, be yourself because you are perfect, stay strong because you can do it, and you are loved by lots and lots of people. Right now I know it's hard with the whole separation process, but when you read this letter, I hope it's better. I hope that Ella is ok and I hope you are ok. Just stay yourself through the good and the bad.

Ethan Sierra

Future

When I grow up I would like to be a lawyer, have a wife and two kids, and continue to be happy.

I would like to be a lawyer so I can help defend innocent people. I would get the job done. I also like to argue my point so the job already suits me plus I have a loud voice so everyone can hear me nice and clear.

When I grow up I would like to have a wife. My wife would be nice and also strong. My kids would be handsome, just like me. My kids would be really athletic and strong.

In the future I would like to continue to be a happy person. Really, who doesn't like to be happy? Also being happy is a great way to start the day. Being happy can make others happy when they are feeling down.

I hope and pray the best for everybody's future and hope it's as good as they want it to be.

Smarlensly Altenor

My Best Moment

The crowd cheering behind me; my teammates screaming my name, the adrenaline rush I'm having. When that ball left my hand, who knew what would happen! I held my breath, then I heard the roar of the crowd. Oh, basketball!

Basketball is my main sport! It's the one that I'm amazing at. My first ever basketball game was when I was six years old. I SHOT THE WINNING BASKET!

Once the ball went through that net, my whole team ran onto the court and lifted me up. Then we all went out and celebrated. We also had cake!

I love playing basketball! I wish you could have been there when I scored that winning basket. IT WAS AWESOME! My coach was so proud of me. The look on her face was indescribable! If you ever think about trying this sport, be sure to write about it so that way I can experience this amazing event with you.

-Smarlensly

Colton Hamilton

My Vacation

Fishing has been a part of my life since I was a toddler. I started fishing in my backyard with my dad when I was two and I have been fishing ever since. Although I enjoy fishing in lakes, I enjoy offshore fishing the best.

My family owns a twenty-four foot sailfish. We have had many good times on our boat. I will never forget our vacation in the Keys. While we were in the Keys, we did a lot of fishing. We caught tons of various snapper. At the end of the day, my friend and I would clean out fish and give it to our parents to cook. Nothing tastes better than fresh fish.

Fishing is a great hobby because you get to spend time with family and friends. Fishing Is also a good way to get some groceries. I love to fish and would do it every day if I could.

Kellen Brown

Dear Kellen,

People have a life to live, and I hope you're living it to the fullest. My goals right now are for you to become a firefighter so you can get a motorcycle. So how's that working out?

Well, we have goals. I don't know how you got the motorcycle, but you got it right? The me right now wants a Ducati or something, and hopefully you can afford it. Also, how's being a firefighter? I hoped you became one so you had time for your bike.

After reading this letter, I hope you consider childhood dreams. Dreams are what set a course for people. I wish you the best of luck, and I am hoping you are living your life to the fullest.

From,

Yourself

Markesha Thompson

Dear Markesha,

I hope mom has let us out of the house by the time you read this. I feel that we would have a good life, great husband, wonderful kids, amazing cars. Did you manage to go to University of Florida like we planned? Are you full of joy and peaceful with the planet? You have to tell me everything!

I know you've been baffled throughout life; I certainly have. Hopefully the future has been filled with brand new technology, real hover boards, flying cars, you know extraordinary technology. Maybe there are holograms where you can FaceTime our friends and seem like we are there in person. It would be fascinating if we made it to Haiti or Jamaica, hopefully both!

The future seems so far, yet so close. Hopefully we are tough enough to get through lawyers or our childhood dreams of becoming an actress. Let the sun shine through the curtains and hits your face because trust your past self. It will happen so quickly that you might forget you wrote this. Can't wait to meet you in person.

Sincerely,
Markesha

Gabby Richards

When I Grow Up

As young adults we still have choices that we have to make, and those choices will include finding an answer to the question "What do you want to be when you grow up?" Despite the fact that this will be a hard decision, it will help tremendously to conceive this idea now rather than later. When I grow up, I wish to be a singer or artist, dancer, actress, lawyer, doctor, or writer. Although these particular jobs require a great amount of hard work and effort, I do believe that I will succeed in obtaining one of these positions in my life.

Being a singer or artist is very much alike to being an actress, but they are different in their own way. A singer/artist is someone who has a job in the music industry. They can write and record their own songs or they can just do one of those procedures; I would love to acquire this job because I love to sing and when you do something that you love, you will never feel like you are at work. Becoming an actress would mean that you would get to transform yourself into someone else. I think that I would be a good actress because I can memorize words with ease, and I think that it would be a great experience to be someone other than myself for a change; being someone else would also allow me to see how others face problems so that I can be prepared for the upcoming difficulties in my life. That's why I would like to be an actress or singer/artist.

Another two jobs I would like to have are writer or lawyer.

These choices are very similar and both call for excellent writing skills. My reason for picking lawyer out of an assortment of other jobs is because I have a lot of experience with arguing and I have gradually developed a talent for winning the arguments that I am involved in. My logic for choosing writer is because I love to write and I'm actually pretty good at it. To make a great essay or report, I have to find a way to get into the right mood, but it really depends on the topic that I'm writing about. Both these positions require a great education, and my current grades show that I can accomplish getting into a good college that allows me to do so.

Even though these jobs are very different, I wouldn't mind being a doctor or a dancer. When I was four years old, I conceived the idea that I was going to be a doctor when I grow up and ever since then that has been one of my goals. I just wanted to follow in my mom's footsteps. I also believe that it would be fun to be a dancer since I have an ear for music and I can dance to the beat of any song. I may not be the best dancer in the world now, but maybe that will change as I get older.

There are a variety of jobs you can choose from when you graduate from college and it will most likely be a difficult decision to make, but it won't be impossible. There will probably even be new jobs in the future that you can look forward to. I want to be a singer or artist, dancer, actress, lawyer, doctor, or a writer, but that's just me.

Sarah Richmond

Dear Future Self,

Here I am, sitting here as a thirteen year old eighth grader. I always dream of my future and what may happen. I hope you are living a happy and successful life. Right now I am finally learning the real definition of life. I've made some mistakes, and I've learned a plethora of lessons. I don't want you to forget that it is okay to only have one true best friend. Many friends will come and go, but there will always be that one true friend that you can always go to.

The thought of me driving and being in charge of my own life gives me chills. I wonder if you love driving as much as you thought you would? Right now I am getting trained for volleyball in high school. Do you still like to play? I really like softball, but they canceled school softball this year so I can't play. Lately, I've been very athletic and I can't wait to play sports in high school.

I am wishing that you love yourself. Do not let others bring you down for how you look or act. The key to happiness is to love yourself. Never ever stop smiling. Stay close to God and make sure you are going to Mass every Sunday. Do you pray every night like you said you would?

I really hope that you find happiness through people and not money. I'm finally starting to realize all of the important people in my life that I couldn't live without. Don't take things for granted. Have an enjoyable life, but don't forget to be there for others like you always are. I love you.

Love,
You as an 8th grader,

Sarah Richmond

Dylan Seissiger

Dear Self,

This is you from the past. The date is November 4, 2015. If you can't remember what you wanted to do when you have grown up, here is a reminder. You wanted to graduate high school and college. You also wanted to get a car.

What I want to do during high school is play lacrosse and become really good at it. I want to join some clubs like the animals club, the building club, get good grades, and learn some Spanish. Lastly, I want to make a lot of friends.

What I want to do during college is get good grades, meet new people, get a great job, and pass all my classes. I want to learn a lot of helpful things that will help me later on in life too. I hope to graduate with a good degree, and I might even buy a house or an apartment after I graduate, if I make enough money with my job.

Finally, I want to get a car. When I get a car I want to drive to a lot of theme parks like Universal and Islands of Adventure, and drive up north to Indiana and Cincinnati, Ohio, to see my relatives. Then, I would drive to all my favorite restaurants. Lastly, I would drive all my friends to places.

Well, that is what I want to do when I grow up. I hope you remember to do those things. If you don't, just read this and you will remember. Make sure to do all those things for me please. Thank you.

Sincerely,

Your past self,

Dylan Seissiger

Bryce Shevak

Florida Gators

Ever since I was little, I have been doing the chomp with the rest of Gator Nation. I've been a Florida Gator from the start and will be for life. Blue and orange runs through my veins. Not only do I watch the games, I sometimes attend them with family and friends. Being a part of Florida football with family and friends is the best thing a fan can experience.

A few years back, my dad started experimenting with BBQ. Now, he makes the most succulent ribs, delectable pulled pork, and the most seasoned of BBQ sauces and rubs. Having barbecue on a Saturday for a Gator game is a tradition now. A tasty one at that. Watching the game at home is fun, but actually going to the Swamp? Now that is awesome. Tailgating, tossing a football, feeling the roar of the crowd when we score is the most thrilling phenomenon a college football fan can have.

Of course being a sports fan, your team goes up and down. A few years ago, we had a bad season. But since then, we have been going up, up, and up. This year so far, the Gators have only one loss on the season. Even on the ups and downs, a true fan stays with their team. With our two biggest rivalry games this year having a big impact on our playoff chances, (Georgia and FSU) it will be a fun second half of the season. The Gators decimated the Bulldogs 27-3.

Growing up watching Tim Tebow win championships, to learning to severely dislike FSU, or just watching my team win, the Florida Gators truly are the best team to cheer and support. From Mister Two Bits to Steve Spurrier, the legacy of the greats will live on. There simply is no other alternative than the blue and orange of the Florida Gators. So I say to you, "Go Gators!"

Bennett Suba

Holiday High-Jinx

The holiday season, that special time of year when smiles go up and money in bank accounts go down. Whether you get to spend Christmas with a lot of people or only a few, everyone finds something to look forward to. What I enjoy the most is getting to see my family and catch up on all that has happened. I always have so much fun on the holidays whether I'm enjoying special Christmas food, fooling around with my older cousins, or opening presents. Sometimes though, we tend to have maybe a little too much fun with each other during the holidays.

Something we can all enjoy around the Christmas season is the Christmas dinner. For my family, we always get together on Christmas Eve and have homemade food made from everyone in the family. Everyone contributes making an epic Christmas feast for us to devour. I remember one year when the desserts were set out and my cousins and I came up with a game. One person would sit at the top of stairs pretending to be "The Boss," while everyone else would take turns choosing a dessert they thought the boss would like. It wasn't until my aunt found out we were taking food upstairs then suddenly, the desserts were off limits.

Everyone loves their family, but the amount of tolerance you have for them isn't always the best. No matter what I always seemed to have an extraordinary amount of fun with my cousins, but when you're the baby of the family, it doesn't always go well. One year we all decided it would be cool to set up a haunted house in the basement. The shrill screams could be heard throughout the house, but the amusement stopped when my cousin Joey somehow got his toe stuck under the basement door. To this day I don't know how it was possible to do that, but lucky for me, I was too scared to go down there and got off scot-free.

It's natural for kids on the holidays to receive presents, whether it is something you really want or would rather avoid completely. It was always our family tradition for the kids to sit in a circle and share the presents they received. Another tradition was The White Elephant Gift for the adults where untagged presents would be in a center pile and each person would take a chance choosing one. What had started as a little joke, turned into an obsession of the family when one year my dad gave a fresh pineapple as the gift. It was based having just moved to Florida and my dad thought it would be funny. Turns out we started a trend that may never ceases to finish.

Every year brings so many new memories. Some of my best memories are from when I spend the holidays with my family. I've always loved spending time with them whether we're sharing a wonderful homemade meal, enjoying each other's company, or opening goofy presents. No matter what, the holidays will always be something special for my family and me.

Kyle Trabulsy

My Bucket List

I have always wanted to go to Hawaii and California to skim board with Austin Keen. I want to adopt three dogs. I want to have four wheeler that turns into a Jet Ski. These are some of the things I would like to do.

Skim boarding can give you an amazing thrill rush. There is a professional skim board person whose name is Austin Keen. I would like to skim board with him in Hawaii and California. You can surf big waves in while skim boarding.

I would like to adopt three dogs. Dogs will have your back during tough times. I already have a dog. I want two Labrador retrievers and one Great Dane. Labradors are great listeners and Great Danes are just massive. It will just be hard taking care of all of them, but these dogs will be your best friend forever.

I want a four wheeler that turns into a Jet Ski. Mudding is always fun, but what if your four wheeler drowned in water? You hit a button and it switches into a Jet Ski . That's amazing, right? What if you can't afford a trailer for your Jet Ski? You can just press a button and it turns into a four wheeler.

This is my bucket list so far. I'm sure my bucket list will get longer as I get older, but for now I will stick with skim boarding, owning three dogs and having a four wheeler that turns into a Jet Ski. Bucket lists are fun to make because you can use your imagination to wish for anything that you'd like to do during your life.

Evan Vanover

Dear Evan,

Oh my goodness, are you actually reading this? Well, that's a miracle. Hey, this is your past self and I hope your goals are coming closer to you each day. I hope that you have gotten a lot better at making the correct decisions. I also wish you have a great energetic family who are all interested into sports especially football. So I hope your new life is going well from your old Eighth grade self.

The reason I'm writing this is because I felt the need to help you out if you were having a bad day. Like your girlfriend dumped you or you lost your car just saying, but I'm sure we both still have our personality. And you probably have faced more problems, but since you're older now you know how to solve them unlike me; I'm still trying to solve them myself. Unlike me you probably have a job and make sure it's a job that suits you okay. When you see this letter please remember to keep your own personality and don't live a life you don't want to.

From,
Your past self-Evan Vanover

Caitlin Kooman

Dear Future Self,

There are many hopes and dreams I have for you right now as an eighth grade student at Saint Anastasia. I hope you are married, have children, and have an amazing job. You are an amazing person and of course, I hope that hasn't changed. I hope you are giving back to the society and helping others.

The first thing is that I hope you are married. I hope you have an amazing husband who is nothing but good to you and your family. The second thing is that I hope you have children. I hope you have one boy and one girl, and they are the most important people in your life. The last thing is that I hope you have an amazing job. I hope it is a great job (hopefully a doctor) that you love going to everyday.

I hope you have an amazing life, and you give your kids and husband an amazing life too. I hope you have a fun life also, not always stuck up in work and business. I hope you are still the great person you are now, and you are loving your adult life.

Love,
Caitlin

Veronica Beckford

My Favorite Memory

Everybody has important memories in their life. Most of them are family trips, or seeing newborn babies for the first time, but mine's not. Mine is the time I helped plan, decorate, and be in my sister's wedding. It was an important time in my life that I will never forget.

I actually got to help plan the wedding. I went to The Island Club on the beach, where the wedding was, and helped my sister decide where things looked best. I talked to the people there, about what was going on and when it was going to happen. I have got to help set up the reception room, with my best friend and my mom. I also have got to help plan the steps in which all of the events were going to happen. I even helped arrange the flowers all around the area.

I have got to help decorate the reception room. It had yellow and teal flowers, with seashells. The cups were mason jars with yellow and teal bottoms, with tags that had beach animals on them, I placed five on each table. The center pieces were turquoise orbs in the bottom of clear vases with big yellow flowers in them. I put one in the middle of each table, and put blue lights around them. I also put big mason jars on the main table, where my sister and her husband were going to sit, there was one for each member of the wedding party.

I was the flower girl in the wedding. My other sister's

baby was the ring bearer, I helped him walk down the aisle with the pillow. I tossed flower petals and seashells in the sand. Then the bridesmaids and my mother walked down the aisle. Finally, it was time for my sister and my father to walk down. My oldest sister and I instantly started crying (luckily I had hidden some tissues in my basket). Her husband started smiling and she giggled, they said their vows and when they kissed, they were together forever.

Being a part of my sister's wedding was a big part of my life. It is one of my best memories. It is definitely one I will never forget.

Alexys Weideman

Traveling Memories

I love traveling with my family. I've gone to many places in my life like Ohio, New Jersey, and even took a road trip all the way from Florida to Canada. I always have so much fun on any road trip.

One of my favorite traveling memories was the road trip from Florida to Cedar Point, Ohio. My family and I love going on roller coasters, so we decided to go to one of the best amusement parks in America. On the way there, I got to see many different places. When we got to Ohio, we were able to ride one of the tallest roller coasters ever built and even one of the fastest. I can't wait to drive to another park or to Cedar Point again!

A couple years ago my family and I had to take a plane ride to New Jersey for Christmas. I was so excited that year because I thought that was going to be the first time I saw snow. When we got to New Jersey the weather forecast said there was going to be no snow at all for Christmas. I was sad, but on the day of Christmas, my spirits were lifted because of all the gifts underneath the tree. That night my brother prayed for snow and surprisingly, a small snow storm came in the next day. My siblings and I were so excited because that meant that we were able to stay for a couple more days. After that we were forced to rent a car and drive all the way back home because no flights were taking off. My first time seeing snow and going to New Jersey was the most unforgettable trip.

The most thrilling trip I went on was when we drove all the way up the east coast from Florida to Niagara Falls, Canada. In Canada we were able to go on many different adventures. My family was able to go right next to the falls on a boat. Another thing we were able to do was able to go underneath the falls and read about all of the people that have attempted to go over the falls. I remember reading about a woman that tried to go over in a barrel or even a little boy who went over with just a life jacket and survived. I loved going to Niagara Falls and I can't wait to go again.

I have traveled many times with my family, and we have visited many places. I have gone to Cedar Point, Ohio, taken a plane ride to New Jersey, and even traveled the east coast to Niagara Falls. Traveling is one of my favorite things to do, and I hope to travel more when I get older.

Quenay N. Woody

Hello Future Me,

Right now I'm in the eighth grade planning for my future, wanting to get married, have an amazing job, and have children. I always thought I should live my life to the fullest and to not let anyone bring me down then my future might be brighter than what I have expected.

I want a husband that would love me more than anything and care for our children. He needs to have a job so he can help pay bills and for food. Being married looks challenging at my age now, but I'm sure everything will be A-OK! I want two or three children one boy and two girls, one boy and one girl, all girls or all boys. I want my children to have an amazing education and start planning for their future just like their mommy!. I would really like for my kids to be athletes, but also balance their school work and sports at the same time. I would always make time for my children, no matter what happens!

Wherever I live I would like a 3/2 or 4/2 house or apartment. I would like two jobs, a part time job and a job that I own, so I have more money to help my children and my home! As my age right now I want to have a lot of money but if I don't a couple hundred would be good! So I really want to live my life so I can see how my future is going to turn out just to be me!!!!

Sincerely, younger version of you,

Quenay N. Woody

P.S. Tell your husband and kids I said hey!

Bryant Melton

Dear Future Self,

I hope you're successful and contributing to society. Please tell me you're still involved with baseball, even if it's not professional. Anyways, I was thinking today and I really hope you aren't stressed. I see what it does to people and I don't want you to be that person. Really though I don't need a lot of money to be satisfied. But I won't be satisfied if you're a bum living under a bridge.

I wish for you to be at least getting by comfortably. I also wish for you to have a nice family of a wife and two kids. When you were my age you always used to say that you were going to raise your kids up being a nice parent, I hope you're fulfilling that. Make sure your kids aren't lazy and spend time with them. Also, if you have a boy, turn him into the next Babe Ruth.

Have a good time with life; I'll see you in the next twenty years or so!

Sincerely,
Your fourteen year old self, Bryant

Matthew Caskey

Dear Matthew,

You may be asking yourself a couple of questions right now. What is this letter? Who is this from? Why does this look like my handwriting? Well believe it or not this is your old self talking to you through a piece of paper. How ironic is that? Me talking to you through a piece of literature? Anyway, this was supposed to be only in a book that your 8th grade teacher told you to do, but I decided to make a copy for you. So go ahead, relive the memories and remind yourself of your future goals.

If you don't have visions of high school or college, that is because this letter was made when you were 8th grade. Just wanted to let you know about that, but I hope you do that on your own. Besides, the memories when you were in middle school were so great. Like, remember the parties you went to. Think of the times in P.E where you scored a stunning free kick for 30 meters out. Those were such great memories and ones that you should definitely tell your kids.

Now, I hope you are physically in shape because I want you to become a soccer or football player. If not, somehow you should be upset given the fact that you practiced so much when you were my age. Putting all of that time and effort to complete an unfinished dream is a massive disappointment. Anyway, I have no idea what you are doing, but I hope it makes you happy and successful. For now enjoy what you are doing and I hope this letter reminded you of your past.

Sincerely,
Yourself

www.ingramcontent.com/pod-product-compliance
Lightning Source LLC
Chambersburg PA
CBHW071640050426

42443CB00026B/777